How to Make F

The Ultimate Guide For Teens

By

Jennifer Love

Table of Contents

Introduction

This book talks about ways for teenagers to meet people and make friendships. Being a teenager is tough – juggling between getting good grades, negative peer pressure, dating and relationship problems, work, media overload, bullying, drug and alcohol addiction, suicide and depression, and communicating with your parents is challenging. And what is important to remember is that the decisions you make as a teenager will affect the rest of your life, so it's best to make them smart decisions.

You'll learn strategies to discover what you want and what you like in life; as well as who you want to hang out with and how to begin successful interactions with these people. Then you can decide whether these people are good or are adding value to your life or not – eventually becoming your lasting friends.

It includes strategies and ways to begin conversations, and the mindset you need to have when meeting new people.

It goes into topics that are common for teenagers such as:

- Discovering what you like and how to find people with similar interests

- How to meet good people because the people you hang out with have the biggest influence on your life – both negative and positive

- Strategies to get along and communicate effectively with your parents and ways to help them understand you

- Self image – how do you see yourself, and how do you want to be seen?

- And much more!

Nine Things You Can Do Today To Start Making Friends

Teenage life can be challenging. As we grow up and slowly learn to make our own decisions toward becoming independent, we are also exposed to a whole new environment, which can be very harsh and confusing. We are expected to figure out a lot of things all at once: who we are, what we want, who our friends are, and what to stay away from. Peer pressure is brutal; we are constantly under the scrutiny of others, made to seek validation from the jury of our peers, and being different will not be easy.

Before you try to get to know other people, you have to get to know yourself. Even adults sometimes forget how important it is to be acquainted with one's self. Discover your own likes and dislikes, strengths and weaknesses, and other important characteristics. The more you know about yourself, the better you can handle interaction with others. It's very important to discover who you are, so that you can use your own characteristics to your advantage. Exercise your own ability to tell right from wrong. Try some new things; trust your own judgment. Find out what you like to do. Once you get validation from yourself, it will be easier for you to gain the approval of other people. Self-confidence is an important and rare commodity in teenagers.

Getting to know your peers doesn't have to be so difficult. To some people, social interaction comes naturally; for others, it can be very uncomfortable and unnatural. There is no exact formula in making friends but there are some tips you can follow.

1) **Be polite and cheerful**. It's always important to make a good first impression. Greet the people you know when you come across them in the corridor. Learn how to say "thank you" and "sorry." Even a little kindness can go a long way and being nice to the people you meet will draw others to you.

2) **Don't be shy**. Don't be afraid to strike conversations with strangers. Ask questions and find out what they like. Share your hobbies.

Learn how to reach out to other people. Try to be interested in what they find interesting. Who knows? You might come to like what you will see.

3) **Find a clique**. Or at least focus on befriending one person at a time. This way, you have a close companion in things you do. It will be easier to choose a partner for laboratory activities and other group work activities. It will help you attain some sense of belongingness in the group of your peers.

4) **Don't pretend to be someone you're not**. Focus on showing your positive characteristics and be yourself. It is important to establish who

you are to your friends. It can be confusing and downright annoying to your friends if they don't know whether or not you're lying to them. People can tell if you're being pretentious and it will make them trust you less.

5) **Project confidence**. This is important especially when you meet someone who doesn't like you. Not everyone you will meet will be friendly and pleasant. Some of your peers are going to be hostile. They will be mean to you; they will say bad things about you behind your back. They will definitely try to humiliate you. You must show them that you can take care of yourself.

6) **Exercise proper timing**. Even the right gestures can come off as awkward and lame, even desperate, when made at the completely wrong moment. Don't be rash. Everything has a right time and place. Avoid doing things that are wildly out of context.

7) **Don't overdo things**. This is one of the most important things you need to know if you want to play it cool. Don't get too carried away with anything. Being too friendly, too outspoken, or too confident might draw too much attention to you. In this phase of your life, this is one thing you want to avoid. Your enemies can use this spotlight to focus on your flaws. It can take months and months to be popular and

respected, but only one social catastrophe can bring that all down. Don't get carried away.

8) **Think carefully of what you post on social networking sites**. A lot of interactions nowadays are done online. Having Facebook, Twitter, and Instagram accounts is highly recommended, if not mandatory. People are very particular with online profiles, and interacting via the Internet also has its own set of rules. Be sure to act accordingly on these sites. Remember tip number seven!

9) **Act intelligently and try to make sense in your decisions**. There is no perfect formula for communicating well with others. Different people will react differently to what you do. And

most importantly, every teenage clique or group has its own rules; learning these rules can help you learn how to act in front of your peers.

Keep in mind that the whole teenage community is like a herd of animals, all mimicking each other's manners and actions. It will be difficult to be the odd-one-out. There are certain rules to follow if you want to fit in. Teenagers usually change their personality repeatedly in their attempts to be part of the group. They try to get good grades, they attempt to improve their sense of fashion, they learn sass and sarcasm and use it well, they listen to the latest music, and they keep track of trends and vogue. *And they engage actively in social networking sites such as Facebook and Twitter.* Wow. That's a lot, isn't it? Just remember: whenever things get tough, you always have the option to take a step back and relax.

Tips To Make Friends

Now that you know the basics of teenage interaction, it's time to focus on making friends. We can't really pick our friends; friendship comes naturally. It is not something that should be contrived artificially. It's easier to be friends with the following kinds of people:

- Someone who has the same interests and hobbies as you do

- You have similar personalities, likes and dislikes.

- You can relate with each other's' experiences.

- Most importantly, you trust each other.

Spend more time with these people to establish a stronger friendship. Hang out whenever you can, wherever you can. Have lunch together and talk about the things you like. Take turns in participating in each other's hobbies. Engage in camaraderie. Try something new together. Go watch a movie. Invite them over to your place. The more activities you do together and the more experiences you share, the closer you will be with your friends.

Friendship is a deep bond that two people share. It is much more meaningful than just experiencing things with others; it is built on mutual trust and regard between people. Learn how to do favors for each other. Share your things with your friends. Keep in mind that your friends will make mistakes, and so will you. It shouldn't be such a big deal. Apologize. Learn how to look past your differences and disappointments and forgive your friends. Speak your mind. Don't let miscommunication or misunderstandings get between your friendships.

Interact with each other online as well. Liking and commenting on each other's status updates is a gesture of support between friends. Post pictures of you together. Pay attention to the content your friends post on the Internet. Read their blogs and chat online. But keep in mind that interaction and communication in real life is much more important than what's online.

Most importantly, keep in mind that friendship is a two-way relationship. Much like the idea of give and take, refrain from allowing yourself to be exploited by others under the misguided definition of friendship. Real friends stick up for each other, support each other, and are there for each other in times of need. And the best of friends look out for each other's interests.

Dealing With People You Don't Like

Not everyone you'll meet will be warm and friendly. Of course, you can't please everyone. You will probably dislike some people as well. It could be mere physical appearances, annoying mannerisms and demeanors, or faults, whether accidental or deliberate, that will cause you to hate certain people. Making enemies is part of maturing emotionally and your teenage years may see a lot of hostility.

Dealing with people you don't like can be time-consuming. Teenagers tend to engage in petty popularity contests everywhere, including the Internet. A lot of people get carried away trying to outshine their enemies. They call each other foul names, throw insults and slander, and pretty much do a lot of immature things against the people they hate. It can get pretty nasty and messy. As much as possible, if you happen to have an enemy who behaves like this, keep your cool. Don't get carried away. Try as much as possible to keep your temper in check. Think things through before you act to avoid making decisions you will regret.

Most teenagers fail to realize that by participating in juvenile fights, they are causing more harm to themselves than their enemies. If you do get carried away, prepare yourself for the consequences. We all make mistakes so we can grow to be better people anyway. Your teenage years are a series of valuable life experiences that will help you develop into a better adult.

On a more serious note, bullying is a major problem in teenage society nowadays. There are many forms of bullying amongst teenagers. Physical bullying, emotional and psychological bullying can devastate their victims. The terrible feeling of helplessness and constant exposure to many kinds of pain a victim of bullying experiences are extremely harmful. In order to cope with such harm, here are a few things that can help you deal with bullying:

- **Seek help**. Find someone you can talk to. Talking to your teachers, your parents, your siblings, and your friends can help you deal with bullying. Tell them exactly what you experienced and tell them how you feel. Don't be afraid of being called a tattle-tale. Expressing your feelings is very important. If you think none of these people will listen to you, seek further help. Search for an anti-bullying hotline. Go to the guidance counselor, or even the principal. There are other people out there who know exactly what you're going through and want to help you. Keep that in mind.

- **Keep it together**. Don't do anything too drastic. It's hard to deal with the constant fear of being bullied. Find healthy ways to express your negative emotions. Listen to music and don't be ashamed of crying. Go take a walk and spend some time alone. Remember that things will pass and eventually, you will pull through this.

- **Stand up to your bullies**. This does not mean you have to strike back at those who are bullying you. This just means you have to get back up every time they strike you down. Do not let them take control of you. Learn how to stick up for yourself during the times when no one else is there for you. You are stronger than you think. They can keep hurting you but they must never own you.

If you know someone who is a victim of bullying, do not hesitate to provide all the emotional support you can give that person. It is also appropriate to inform the adults around you of this bullying.

If, on the other hand, you are the bully, then seek help from the responsible adults as well. Do not fear punishment. What people fail to understand is the people who administer bullying are just as in need of help as the victims of bullying. Please take some time to understand the magnitude of damage you are causing to the people you are bullying. Do not hesitate to ask for help as well.

Sad Times Will Come & Go

Self-preservation is very important during your teenage years. Between dealing with an entirely new environment and the endless socializing, maintaining a good reputation, bullying, striving to get good grades, and engaging in various extra-curricular activities, teenagers can be hard-pressed to find time for themselves. You might find yourself dealing with depression and fatigue. A few symptoms of depression include:

- Having trouble sleeping at night
- Waking up tired
- Frequent sighing

- Having a fondness for violence in television shows and films

- Losing interest in things you like

- Overall lack of sense of accomplishment in things you strive for

Depression is not simply feeling sad when something in your life goes wrong. Kevin Breel, in his short video talk, defines depression as being sad when everything in your life is going right. Everything you do simply wears you out and you're tired of all that; you might not even be aware of it.

Dealing with depression can be very difficult. Many people are simply unaware that they are suffering from depression; they just attribute it to other things and don't take it seriously. People with depression fail to regard their lives as important and inflict self-harm, consciously or not. They are haunted by their own negative thoughts and insecurities, and our society forces them to put on a brave face and smile on the surface. They are subjected to so much emotional isolation and loneliness that they lose the ability to appreciate the good things in life.

Society can be really cruel and indifferent to people with depression. They are labeled as over-sensitive and attention-seeking, even crazy. Depression must be taken seriously and there are a few methods to mitigate its effects:

- **Take a day off from your usual routine; rest if necessary**. One day without posting any updates on Facebook, without stressing too much on school work. One day without watching your usual TV shows or worrying about your diet. Let go of all the weight you carry, even just for a day.

- **Set some time for yourself**. Find a hobby only for you. Keep it a secret. It could be playing a video game, or reading a book. Or staying in your own secret haven. Visit a pet store. Collect stamps or other novelty items. Ride the loop train for three whole laps. Do something silly.

Wander in a different town. Ride a Ferris wheel at night and take a look at the world from the very top. Lie down on the roof or in any place you can and look at the stars and ponder how silly it is to worry too much about the little things in life.

- **Write about it**. Keep a little notebook and write "I feel sad," or "I can't take it anymore." Write about how hard it is. Keep that notebook to yourself. It's a secret. Write and write until you're no longer sad.

- **Refrain from overexerting yourself.** Keep yourself fit and healthy by making exercising a habit. The truth is the only person you can rely on all the time is yourself. Get yourself back to fighting shape. Whatever failures you encountered previously are not going to affect how well you can do in the future. Keep in mind that life isn't a race, and success does not mean getting there first.

If you are still dealing with severe depression and sadness, don't give up. Wait for things to get better. Do what you have to do to cope. If there is a source of stress that won't go away, find a healthy way of handling it. Learn how to forgive yourself and accept the things you cannot change.

Solutions To The Confusion Between Teens & Parents

The relationship between teenagers and their parents can be very complicated and confusing to both parties. Most teenagers are in their rebellious phase in life, eager to try the many new things exposed to them. They see their parents hitting on the breaks as hindrances, holding them back from enjoying their youth. They try to negotiate the rules, pushing curfews forward and asking for bigger allowances. They start making comparisons between lenient parents and strict parents. They learn to lie to their parents. They learn to blatantly disobey their parents just to have their way.

From your parents' point of view, it is equally appalling. Their little kid has now turned into an impertinent stranger who answers back and refuses to take out the trash. They are having great difficulty accepting the fact that their child has begun to mature into a young adult and is starting to learn how to decide for his/her own self. In reaction to this, they try to assert their control over their children again, sometimes excessively. As a result, the miscommunication and misunderstanding between the parents and their teenage sons and daughters cause them to start to grow apart. Despite this, there are some ways that might help you have a better relationship with your parents.

1. **Never stop communicating**. Parents feel left out when their child stops communicating with them. As their children get older, they talk less and less to their parents and become isolated. When you stop telling your parents about your day, it bothers them. It bothers them that they have no idea what might be bothering you. Most teenagers come home, march straight up into their room, hardly even acknowledging their mom and dad, and slam the door. This behavior is very confusing and agitating to the parents. Start talking to them again about school, your friends, and what is going on with your life so that they can understand you better.

2. **Act mature and be responsible**. A lot of teenagers complain about how they're still being treated like kids. Your parents are simply treating you the way you act. If they see you making all the wrong decisions, they can hardly treat you like a mature individual. Most teenagers abuse their freedom too much; thus, their parents still decide for them. Show them that you can manage your time and freedom responsibly and maybe they will start treating you like a young adult. Otherwise, you'll always be "too young for that."

3. **Keep in mind that while you're growing up, your mom and dad are growing old**. There is an age gap between you and your parents. Some of your habits will strike them as weird and unethical. Some of their habits will strike you as lame and obsolete. They grew up in an entirely different culture from what you grew up in. Learn how to look past these differences to foster a good relationship with your parents.

4. **Understand that they want to keep you away from bad influences**. Teenagers aren't expected to understand or believe that their parents simply want what's best for them. Your

parents know the dangers of being exposed to vices and other bad things far more than you do, so perhaps it is a good idea to trust their judgment. Taking a closer look, they would actually prefer that you hate them rather than you allow yourself to be led astray.

5. **Your parents are NOT lame.** Whatever they say or do and however "uncool" they may seem by the standards of your peers, your parents are awesome. Your mom and dad have been through so much more. They know much more and they are much wiser. They took care of you when you were little and have been working

hard to provide for you ever since. You should be proud of them, regardless.

In summary, it is very inappropriate to impose the standard of your peers to your parents. To bridge the age gap, both must look past the differences of your respective generations. Try to understand and compromise. Communicate. Always know your place; they are your parents and you should respect their decisions. You and your parents are supposed to be on the same side; your side.

Avoid These People!

A part of being a teenager is the exposure to many new things. A lot of these things are good like sports and clubs. Some things, however, are downright harmful. Things such as alcohol, drugs, cigarettes, tattoos, and engaging in sexual activities can lead to irreversible consequences.

A lot of teenagers succumb to peer pressure and get involved in these things. Teenagers who are desperate to fit in and be accepted into a group will do anything. Perhaps a bunch of misguided youth has decided to christen these bad things as cool or "in", and the desire to belong has impaired their sense of judgment.

Teenagers are hardly expected to follow the advice of grown-ups to stay away from alcohol and drugs, to refrain from smoking, and to stay celibate, particularly if they can see these grown-ups getting drunk and smoking, etc. Teenagers listen to their peers, and while some of their peers are bad influences, some aren't. Take a closer look at your friends who are able to steer free from these bad influences. Listen to their reasons. Keep in mind that you might pay for the rest of your life for a mistake you made in your youth.

When being pestered or pressured to try these bad things, respectfully disagree. Do not say things like

"My mom told me to stay away from that," as it will only make the other person more aggressive. Do not give in to their taunts and jeers. Learn to control yourself. This is not the right time for you to be trying all these things yet. Take a closer look at the people who have already engaged in those kinds of activities. Are they really any happier? Or are they simply using the alcohol and cigarettes and drugs as a distraction to cover up some bigger problem they have?

A better way to avoid being badgered into trying these things is to shun those bad influences entirely. Do not hang out with people who indulge themselves in these illicit activities. Avoid attending parties without responsible adult supervision. Never stop saying no;

there is nothing to be curious about these substances.

Be responsible and your future self will thank you.

Love, Dating, and Relationships

There are a billion sayings about love. Each person has his or her own definition of what love should be. During your teenage years, you will meet a lot of attractive people. You might even have a lot of crushes. You might decide to pursue a person you like. Now keep in mind that different people have different opinions about love. Some people are afraid of commitment. Some people take relationships more seriously than others do. Other people can have other priorities. Some people have no idea how it is to be in a relationship. Others are afraid of getting hurt. And when you're still less than two decades old, it goes without saying that you haven't really figured out who you want to be and what you really want out of life.

Teenagers are often far too eager to find their special partner in life. It can take a while for people to start letting their feelings of attraction show. Some will get rejected, some won't even be taken seriously, and others will simply end up badly. But after several weeks or months of flirting and reading between the lines, you may find someone who reciprocates your attraction to him or her and may decide to start being in a relationship.

It is very complicated to be in a teenage relationship. Both you and your partner are still growing emotionally, are constantly subjected to change, and haven't really figured out what both of you want in life. Often, teenagers say things they don't really understand and make promises they don't mean. And they can't help it.

You enter your first relationship innocent and vulnerable. And it will be exhilarating and perfect, without any sign of trouble. You will both carelessly exchange the phrase "I love you" and it will feel like every love song in the world is about you. Things will seem very smooth and natural at first, but at some point, both of you may grow weary or bored of your relationship. There is a high tendency to demand more excitement and satisfaction from your partner and both of you might end up getting hurt. You will have your first fight, and it will be devastating and unsettling. One or both of you might end up rashly saying something horrible that will end the relationship. But you will learn how to compromise.

Girls and boys communicate and interpret many things differently. Girls like to talk about their feelings; they remember every small detail of the time you spend together and they keep communicating between the lines. They can say one thing and mean the opposite, which can be very confusing to others. When they fall silent, it usually means something is wrong. Some girls complain a lot and make a fuss over many things. They generally take fashion and their figures more seriously than boys do, and are into a lot of things that boys generally cannot relate to such as gossiping. But behind all these, girls can be very affectionate, even possessive of their partner. Most of them are highly jealous and clingy partners. Don't be mistaken: they trust their partner immensely. They just have difficulty watching him or her spend time with other people they identify as potential rivals.

Guys on the other hand are said to be less sensitive than girls. They like to keep things simple and they speak their mind. They are generally more into sports and video games than girls. They have difficulty expressing their thoughts and rarely have much to say about things. Guys are not experts in reading the hidden meanings in the gestures of girls, which commonly leads to fights. They are often accused of taking their female partners for granted. Girls often call guys insensitive because of their failure to notice a girl's distress. Guys are also more private than girls. Guys don't really want to talk about their secrets a lot, so when a girl shares a lot about herself, she becomes uncomfortable and hurt that the guy does not. Guys also forget the important dates sometimes, which greatly offend the girls they are dating.

Because of all these, teenage relationships are prone to misunderstanding. Nevertheless, there are some tips that guys and girls can follow to help them understand each other:

- **There are boyish girls and girly guys**. Deal with the differences. Although stereotypes tend to generalize all people, everyone has their own perks and shortcomings as individuals.

- **Guys, pay more attention to your female partners**. Take interest in the things they find interesting. If they are acting unnaturally, learn how to ask them what's wrong. Listen to what they say. Be more thoughtful and sensitive to girls. Remember the things your girlfriends tell you.

- **Girls, give your male partners some space and privacy**. They are not as fond of opening up as you are. Don't demand too much time from them. Let them engage in their hobbies and interests. And try not to make such a big deal of their lack of responses. Try to take a closer look. Perhaps your boyfriend has been expressing his affection in some way you haven't noticed yet.

- **Establish a strong relationship online**. As with friendships, many people take their online romantic relationship very seriously. Display affection through online interaction such as posting pictures of the two of you together and expressing feelings through social media.

- **Learn to meet each other halfway**. This means accepting the characteristics of your partners, even the ones you don't like. It means changing yourself to be a better boyfriend or girlfriend. Letting someone into your life can make you feel vulnerable and uncomfortable and it is up to you to decide whether or not things are worth it.

You must try and get to know yourself and your partner as you progress in your relationship. Find out your partner's strengths and weaknesses and be the person he or she needs. One of the two secrets to a long-lasting relationship is chemistry. Chemistry refers to how well two people get along; how two people can bring out the best in each other. People with chemistry complement each other's strengths and compensate for each other's weaknesses. The second secret to a relationship that will go the distance is mutual trust. It's how two people never give up on each other, no matter how bad it gets. And it can get pretty bad. The more invested you are in a relationship, the more vulnerable you are. But it's sweet how some people manage to fix things every time, instead of throwing them away.

Remember that people can fall in and out of love given enough time. Learn how to distinguish love from strong infatuation and obsession. Also it may seem that our whole worlds are falling apart during our teenage years, but the truth is all this will pass and we will have our whole lives ahead of us as we become mature adults.

Conclusion

During your teenage years, you will make a lot of mistakes but that is part of life and it will happen no matter what. You might break a lot of rules and make the wrong enemies. You might screw up your relationship with your parents. You might love the wrong person and get horribly hurt, resenting the experience. You might make all the wrong choices and end up altogether unpopular and secluded. You will act like many other teenagers do: painfully eager to be in control, yet mostly clueless about the rules of real life. As of now, you are a small prototype of the person you are going to grow up as. Some of the people you will meet will just pass by your life. Some are there to stay. Many people meet their greatest, closest friends during their teenage years and if you're one of those lucky people, hold on to those friends.

But all this will be part of discovering who we are and who we want to be. The bad things will pass eventually, so don't dwell too much on what you can't change. All the pain coming from growing up will help us develop better judgment. As a teenager, you are still too young to know how you want to live your life. It will be a rough road with emotional, social, and psychological ups and downs. It will be an exciting adventure, perhaps even too exciting at times. Remember to keep getting up and keep smiling, as the best years of your life are yet to come. Many of us will have humiliating memories of adolescence, but when you grow older, you will learn to laugh at all the wild things you did as a teenager.

Made in the USA
Coppell, TX
26 October 2020